# WAY

# DOWN

# BELOW

# DEEP

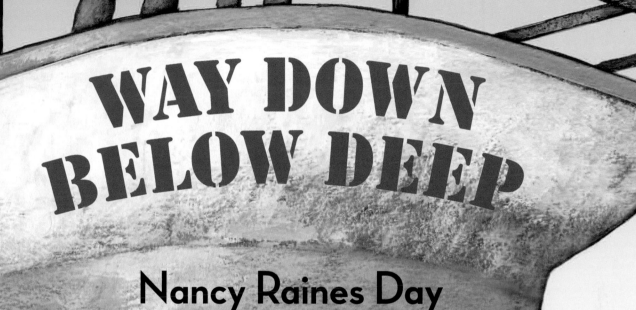

# WAY DOWN BELOW DEEP

## Nancy Raines Day

### Art by David Sheldon

PELICAN PUBLISHING COMPANY

Gretna 2014

Way down below deep, where the sun never goes,
Imagine the creatures that nobody knows.
Though deep sea fills up most of Earth's total space,
We're just finding out about life in this place.

From depths black as ink peer the world's largest eyes.
Have you seen a car's hubcap? They're much the same size.
Yet a GIANT SQUID's eyes should not cause such a fuss
On a body that's longer than any school bus.

my schoolbus

the colossal squid may be even bigger than the giant squid.

the fangtooth has special padding in its mouth so its teeth don't stick into its brain.

The FANGTOOTH does not find its small prey by seeing
But senses the water stirred up by fish fleeing.
This curious creature won't get by on looks.
Instead, his big fangs let him spear food on hooks.

Lanternfish have very large eyes for their size—the better to see in the dark.

In the dark, silent waters these creatures call home,
Most residents carry a light of their own.
These LANTERNFISH headlights give quite an assist.
They flip on their high beams, and mates can't resist.

Deep-sea anglerfish can also walk on the ocean with fins like feet.

She's a great fisherwoman! One female anglerfish may carry several mates.

The ANGLERFISH fishes
with light as her bait.
She snatches her catch
while she's lying in wait.
Her mate is so very much
smaller than she,
He hooks on with his mouth
so he's not lost at sea.

It's like catching moths underwater.

this octopus's suckers don't hold onto things — they glow! that's why it's called a glowing sucker octopus.

This OCTOPUS twists up and stretches, and shrinks,
So predators get so confused, they can't think.
Tiny crustaceans are drawn to its glow.
They stick to its net and cannot let go.

Though oxygen's plentiful up near the air,
In deepest of oceans, there's not much to spare.

the vampire squid eats stinking bits of dead bodies, poop, and snot. Eeww!

this vampire is NOT a predator!

The blood of this vampire doesn't need much
Since squids use it wisely – for living and such.

Sharks, crabs, and more feed on a whale's meat for ten years to expose the bones of the skeleton to whale worms.

Occasionally whale bones sink down to the floor,
And furnish fine food for a century or more!

The bones sprout some "palm trees" – really WHALE WORMS.
With bones of this size, worms don't have to take turns.

Way down below deep, it's so cold plants can't bud,
But SEA PIGS or CUCUMBERS graze on rich mud.

Are they animal? Vegetable? Borders are blurred.
So here is a hint – they move in a herd.

From vents in the bottom pours liquid so hot
That nothing could live there – at least, it should not!
Yet here there are creatures incredibly strange.
They make themselves truly at home on their range.

As chemicals rise up in rotten-egg fumes,
    They're grabbed up by TUBE WORMS with gigantic plumes.
We thought that no food could be made without sun
    But here in the dark, smelly fumes get it done!

smells like rotten eggs!

tube worms can grow taller than a man in a few years.

Bacteria inside these creatures and out
Make sugar from chemicals – plenty about.
These miniature factories feed multitudes –
Snails, clams, and mussels fill up with good food.

In the deepest of depths, so much water's on top,
It's like hippos on every square inch start to hop.
That intense kind of pressure would crush you and me,
Yet creatures with bodies like jelly float free.

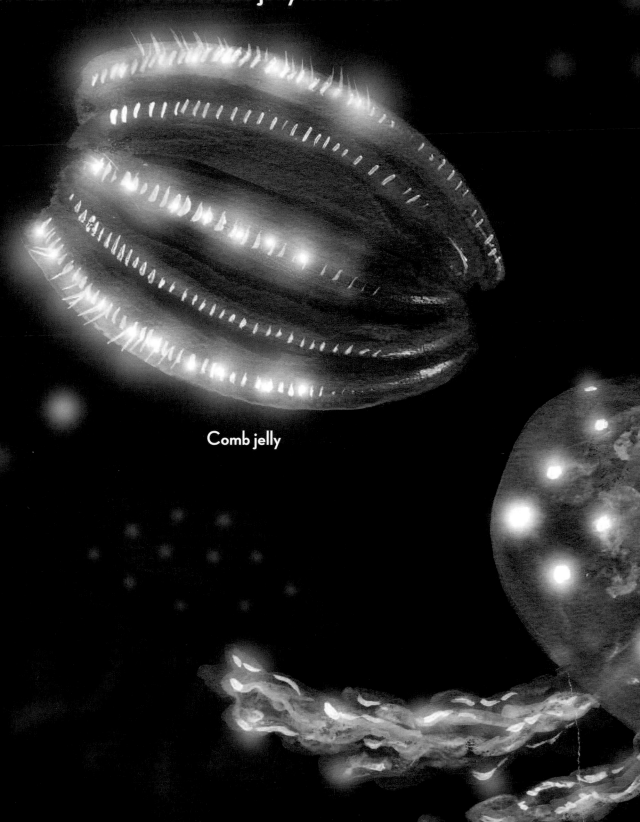

Comb jelly

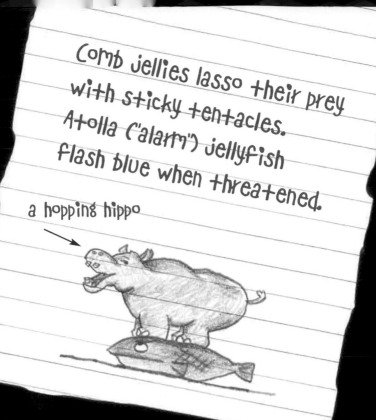

Comb jellies lasso their prey with sticky tentacles. Atolla ("alarm") jellyfish flash blue when threatened.

a hopping hippo

Atolla (alarm) jellyfish

Medusa jellyfish

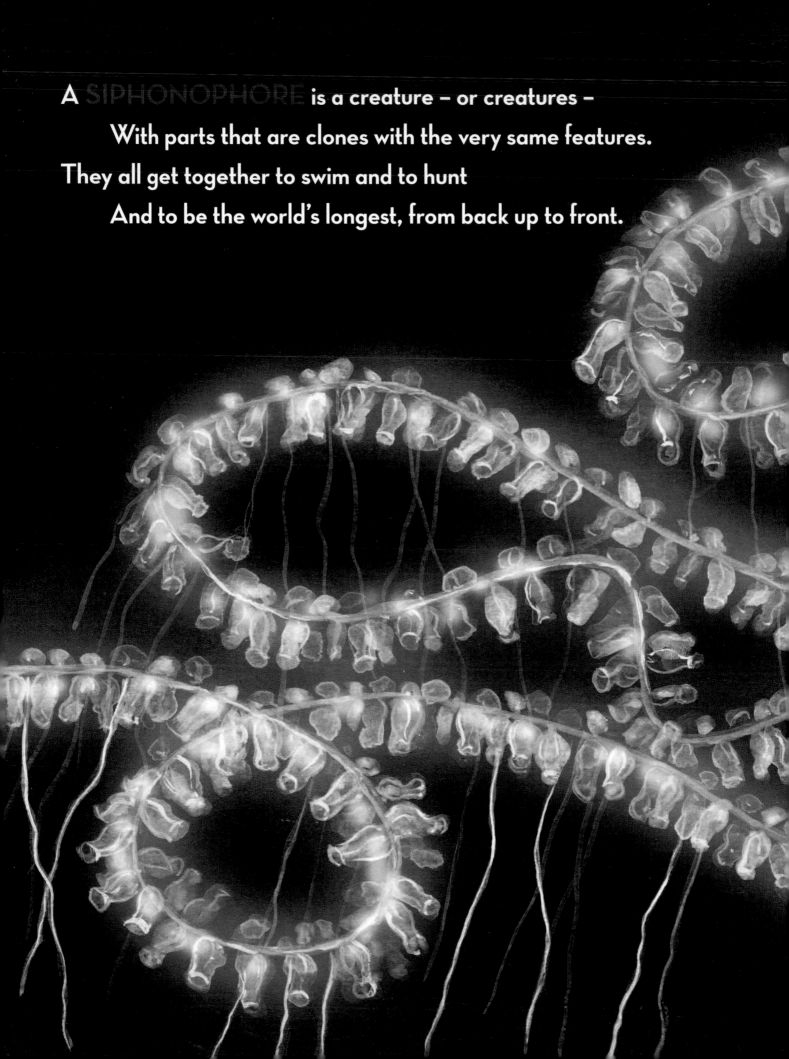

A SIPHONOPHORE is a creature – or creatures –
With parts that are clones with the very same features.
They all get together to swim and to hunt
And to be the world's longest, from back up to front.

looks like my puzzle pieces!

some parts of the giant siphonophore catch prey, some eat, and some swim.

Now, lights, camera, action! The deep sea's revealed.
These creatures are not just imagined – they're real.
All sorts of new species – ten million or more –
Won't even have names till we look and explore!

# Discoveries in the Deep

Researchers are using ROVs (remotely operated vehicles) to observe deep-sea creatures in action for the first time.

• No one had ever seen a live **giant squid** until 2013. One was filmed swimming and eating using lights neither squids nor humans can see.

• The **fangtooth** can't see well with its small eyes. But it can sense movement and vibration in the water around it.

• **Lanternfish** spend the day in the deep and swim up toward the surface to feed at night.

• Deep-sea **anglerfish** turn from blue to red as they get older. They can stow their fishing lure in a space between their eyes.

• The **glowing sucker octopus** doesn't have much to hold onto above the ocean floor. So its hundreds of suckers glow and twinkle instead.

• The **vampire squid** is one of the few squids that is NOT a predator. Instead it drifts to save energy.

• **Whale worms** may take up to 100 years to dissolve a whale skeleton. Whale worms are also called bone or zombie worms, or sometimes palm worms.

• **Sea cucumbers** are scavengers, like earthworms on land. In Asia, people eat them.

• Chemosynthesis is a four-step process: (1) Energy comes from heat from inside the earth, instead of the sun. (2) Chemicals in the smoke combine with water, (3) allowing bacteria to produce sugars. (4) Sulfur (which smells like rotten eggs) is given off.

• **Tube worms**' red plumes are full of blood, which carries chemicals to bacteria inside their tube.

• **Comb jellies** swim by beating rows of combs that light up like a rainbow.

• **Atolla jellyfish**'s "alarm" attracts bigger predators that may eat whatever is threatening it.

• The **giant siphonophore** can be more than 130 feet long. Out of the water, it explodes into its separate pieces.

To Ken, with deepest love. —N.R.D.

Designed by Pinafore Press / Janice Shay

Art for journal entries by Sarah Sheldon: pp. 1, 7, 8, 10, 12, 14, 17, 18, 21, 23, 24, 27, 29

---

---

ISBN: 9781455619450

E-book ISBN: 9781455619467

Printed in Malaysia
Published by Pelican Publishing Company, Inc.
1000 Burmaster Street, Gretna, Louisiana, 70053